EXPLORING FEELINGS: ANXIETY
training manual

A Guide For Group Leaders

— by —

Helen Taylor

Vicki Grahame

Helen McConachie

Ann Le Couteur

Jacqui Rodgers

Jan O'Neill

Ann Ozsivadjian

Emma Honey

Kate Sofronoff

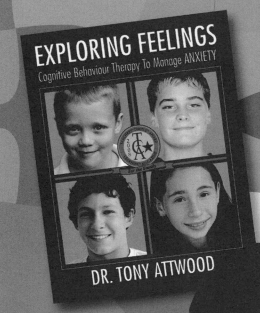

EXPLORING FEELINGS
Cognitive Behaviour Therapy To Manage ANXIETY

DR. TONY ATTWOOD

Foreword by Tony Attwood, PhD

Exploring Feelings: Anxiety Training Manual

All marketing and publishing rights guaranteed to and reserved by:

FUTURE HORIZONS INC.

721 W. Abram Street
Arlington, TX 76013
(800) 489-0727
(817) 277-0727
(817) 277-2270 (fax)
E-mail: info@fhautism.com
www.fhautism.com

Cover & interior design by John Yacio III

ISBN: 9781941765555

Acknowledgement

This guide arises from a research study commissioned by the National Institute for Health Research (NIHR) under the Research for Patient Benefit program (PB-PG-0408-16069). The views expressed are those of the authors and not necessarily those of the NHS, the NIHR or the Department of Health.

Contents

Contents

Foreword

Children who have an Autism Spectrum Disorder (ASD) appear to be vulnerable to feeling anxious for much of their day at home and at school, often experiencing extreme anxiety in anticipation of, or in response to, specific events—such as the sound of a dog barking, making a mistake, or a change in the schedule of activities for the day. Sometimes, the level of anxiety may be perceived by parents and teachers as actually more disabling than the diagnostic characteristics of ASD.

All types of anxiety disorder are more frequent in children with ASD in comparison with typical children; they include specific phobias, Obsessive Compulsive Disorder (OCD), Social Anxiety Disorder (SAD), Generalized Anxiety Disorder (GAD), and Separation Anxiety (Van Steensel et al. 2011). However, there can be qualitative differences in the presentation of anxiety in children with ASD when compared with typical children. Phobias may develop as a response to sensory sensitivity. For example, to particular sounds—such as vacuum cleaners, electric hand dryers, or thunder (Mayes et al. 2013)—which may elicit painful responses with a resultant phobia of these sounds and situations where they can occur. An assessment of the circumstances associated with heightened levels of anxiety can indicate an intolerance of uncertainty (Wigham et al. 2015), as well as a fear of making an error, or performance anxiety (Attwood 2006). There can also be a fear of being targeted for bullying, teasing, rejection, humiliation, and anxiety associated with changes in routine or expectations (Attwood 2006). Socializing with peers is perhaps the greatest source of anxiety.

Anxiety can frequently be associated with specific social situations, such as those circumstances where there are no apparent or previously experienced social rules, or where the social codes or conventions are being deliberately broken by other children. There can be anxiety associated with complex and possibly novel social situations, such as birthday parties, and performance anxiety in terms of being able to apply learned social responses and behavior in real life social settings. The high level of anxiety experienced in social situations, such as the classroom or playground, may result in the child's use of coping strategies that lead to a diagnosis of Separation Anxiety, where the child genuinely needs guidance and reassurance from a parent; and Selective Mutism (in terms of the flight, fight, and freeze response to anxiety), where the child "freezes" and is unable to speak in the classroom, but is verbally fluent when relaxed at home.

The extensive research on Theory of Mind skills and autism confirms that children with autism have considerable difficulty identifying and conceptualizing the thoughts and feelings of both other people and themselves. The interpersonal and inner world of emotions appears to be uncharted territory for children who have autism. This program provides guidance in exploring emotions and is designed to improve the child's ability to monitor and manage anxiety throughout their day.

Another characteristic associated with autism is alexithymia, namely a diminished vocabulary of words to describe emotions; this includes one's own emotions as well as the emotions of other people (Berthoz and Hill 2005; Hill et al. 2004; Samson et al. 2012). Research suggests that the child with autism can identify having an increased level of emotional arousal, but has great difficulty labelling and eloquently describing the level of emotion (Ketelaars et al. 2016). When asked how they are feeling at a particular time or during a particular event, the child with ASD may reply, "I don't know," which means, "I don't know how to tell you." The child may therefore have difficulty telling a teacher or parent how anxious they feel and why they are anxious. However, it may be possible to identify specific behaviors, actions, and thoughts that serve as a behavioral "code" or "clue" for a particular feeling and the depth of that feeling.

The teacher or parent must be a detective or scientist observing, collecting, and analyzing the data regarding which situations and events can precipitate intense anxiety. A new way of exploring and discovering the various levels of anxiety during the day, and the level of anxiety in response to a particular situation, can be sports technology. That is, devices worn on the wrist to measure heart rate, which can be used to record general anxiety levels throughout the day and the level of response to specific situations. The devices can also be used to encourage the ability to relax, using a relaxation strategy such as breath control, where the child is able to observe and respond to the gradual reduction in his or her heart rate.

Deeper levels of relaxation can be achieved using the many different meditation techniques. In Western cultures, there is a growing awareness and appreciation of the value of activities such as yoga in encouraging a general sense of well-being and providing an antidote to anxiety. We now have yoga activities specifically developed for children with ASD to use at school and home (Betts and Betts 2006; Bolls and Sewell 2013; Mitchell 2014; Hardy 2015), and some teachers are now using classroom and individual meditation activities to encourage relaxation and enhanced attention for the whole class. Mindfulness is also being used for children with ASD in school settings to regulate attention toward the present moment, to let an emotion pass and encouraging an attitude of openness and acceptance using imagery, meditation, and yoga (De Bruin et al. 2015).

The original Exploring Feelings program for anxiety was published in 2004, and we have learned so much since then. This new training manual provides a valuable review and update to further explore and manage anxiety for children with Autism Spectrum Disorder.

— **Dr. Tony Attwood, author** (*Exploring Feelings: Anxiety: Cognitive Behaviour Therapy to Manage Anxiety* and *Exploring Feelings: Anger: Cognitive Behaviour Therapy to Manage Anger*)

References

Attwood, T. 2006. *The Complete Guide to Asperger's Syndrome*. London: Jessica Kingsley Publishers.

Berthoz, S., and E.L. Hill. 2005. "The validity of using self-reports to assess emotion regulation abilities in adults with autism spectrum disorder". *European Psychiatry*, 20(3): 291-298.

Betts, D. E., and S.W. Betts. 2006. *Yoga for Children with Autism Spectrum Disorders: A Step-by-Step Guide for Parents and Caregivers*. London, Jessica Kingsley Publishers.

Bolls, U. D., and R. Sewell. 2013. *Meditation for Aspies: Everyday Techniques to Help People with Asperger Syndrome Take Control and Improve Their Lives*. London: Jessica Kingsley Publishers.

De Bruin, E. I., R. Blom, F.M. Smit, F.J. Van Steensel, and S.M. Bögels. 2015. "MYmind: Mindfulness training for Youngsters with autism spectrum disorders and their parents." *Autism*, 19(8): 906-914.

Hardy, S. T. 2014. *Asanas for Autism and Special Needs: Yoga to Help Children with their Emotions, Self-Regulation and Body Awareness*. London. Jessica Kingsley Publishers.

Hill, E., S. Berthoz, and U. Frith. 2004. "Brief report: Cognitive processing of own emotions in individuals with autistic spectrum disorder and in their relatives." *Journal of Autism and Developmental Disorders*, 34(2): 229-235.

Ketelaars, M. P., A. Mol, H. Swaab, and S. van Rijn. 2016. "Emotion recognition and alexithymia in high functioning females with autism spectrum disorder." *Research in Autism Spectrum Disorders*, 21: 51-60.

Mayes, S. D., S.L. Calhoun, R. Aggarwal, C. Baker, S. Mathapati, S. Molitoris, and R.D. Mayes. 2013. "Unusual fears in children with autism." *Research in Autism Spectrum Disorders*, 7(1): 151-158.

Mitchell, C. 2013. *Mindful Living with Asperger's Syndrome: Everyday Mindfulness Practices to Help You Tune in to the Present Moment*. London. Jessica Kingsley Publishers.

Samson, A. C., O. Huber, and J.J. Gross. 2012. "Emotion regulation in Asperger's syndrome and high-functioning autism." *Emotion*, 12(4): 659-665.

Van Steensel, F. J., S.M. Bögels, and S. Perrin. 2011. "Anxiety disorders in children and adolescents with autistic spectrum disorders: a meta-analysis." *Clinical Child and Family Psychology Review*, 14(3): 302.

Wigham, S., J. Rodgers, M. South, H. McConachie, and M. Freeston. 2015. "The interplay between sensory processing abnormalities, intolerance of uncertainty, anxiety and restricted and repetitive behaviours in autism spectrum disorder." *Journal of Autism and Developmental Disorders*, 45(4): 943-952.

Introduction

The aim of this manual is to pass on experience to people wishing to use the Exploring Feelings (Atwood 2004) materials in a group setting with young people who have ASD and high anxiety. We have collated our experience from running groups in a number of different settings, and suggest practical issues to be considered by organizers. The main message is, "Do it!"

The manual is written with the expectation that group leaders will have support from an experienced supervisor. Their experience ought to include a background in Cognitive Behavior Therapy, work with young people with autism spectrum disorder and their families, and child mental health, more generally. The manual is intended as an adjunct training resource for the supervisor and the group leaders. It is written to accompany the Exploring Feelings manual, so it does not repeat information about the tasks and activities.

1 Background to *Exploring Feelings*

Anxiety in Autism Spectrum Disorders

There have been many estimates of the rate of anxiety experienced by young people with ASD. In clinical settings, referrals for anxiety-based problems are among the most common for young people with ASD (de Bruin et al. 2007; Ghaziuddin 2002). A recent meta-analysis found that an average of 40% of children with ASD would meet criteria for an anxiety disorder (van Steensel, Bogels, and Perrin 2011). These rates significantly exceed the prevalence of anxiety among "typically developing" young people, and many young people with ASD present with more than one type of anxiety.

Many of the difficulties faced by young people with ASD are exacerbated, if not caused, by anxiety. It may be that behaviors interpreted as non-compliance or anger are a manifestation of anxiety (e.g., a young person's refusal to leave a classroom and go to the playground). For some children the school setting can be especially anxiety-provoking. Indeed, teacher reports of anxiety frequently reflect greater severity than parent reports (Guttman-Steinmetz et al. 2010). The relationship between anxiety and repetitive behaviors is a subject of ongoing research (Gadow et al. 2010; Wood and Gadow 2010). Some findings suggest that anxiety is likely to exacerbate repetitive and stereotypic behaviors (Joosten, Bundy, and Einfeld 2009). Severe anxiety symptoms and behaviors significantly contribute to the impaired social interaction demonstrated by these young people (Beaumont and Sofronoff 2008), potentially increasing their vulnerability to bullying and teasing from peers among other risks (Sofronoff, Dark, and Stone 2011).

So, young people with ASD are more likely to experience anxiety. The difficulties that they present with in terms of their ASD are likely to be exacerbated by anxiety. An intervention addressing anxiety in this group must accommodate the underlying presentation of ASD.

Introduction to Cognitive Behavioral Therapy

In order to successfully run the Exploring Feelings group, it is helpful to have a basic understanding of the principles of Cognitive Behavioral Therapy (CBT). CBT looks at how you think (cognitions), feel, and behave. It is based on the assumption that feelings (physical and emotional) and behavior are primarily a product of thoughts, and therefore, changing the way you think and behave can lead to changes in how you feel (Kendall 1991). An example of this can be seen in Figure 1 below.

Figure 1. Model of CBT

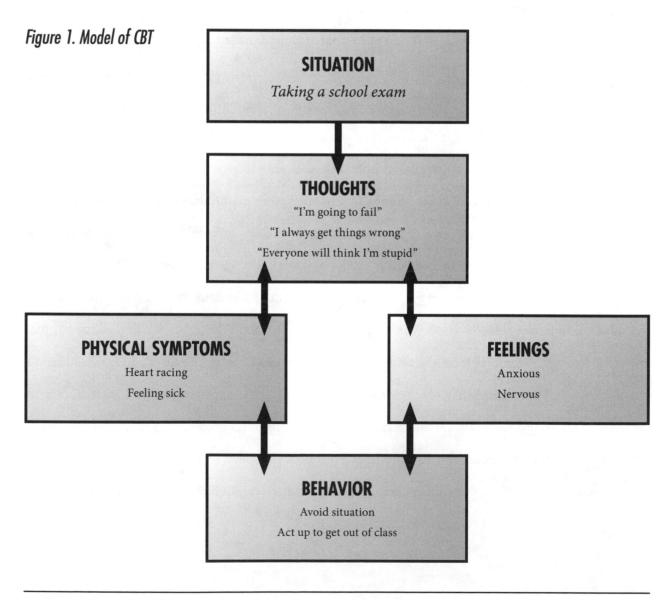

CBT uses cognitive and behavioral interventions to challenge a person's thoughts and behavior and bring about a change in their feelings. Although CBT is used to refer to a wide range of interventions, there are a number of underlying core features which are central to CBT:

- Collaborative process: The individual, along with the therapist, takes an active role in the therapeutic process, learning to recognize their unhelpful thoughts, feelings, and behaviors, and actively challenging these using a range of techniques.

- Time-limited: The focus is on promoting independence and empowering the individual to understand their difficulties and "help themselves".

- Structured: The sessions are structured using an agenda which sets out what the session aims to achieve with the goals of the intervention clearly stated.

- Focus on the here and now: The focus is on the present difficulties the individual is experiencing.

- Focus on skill-building: The focus of the intervention is to help the individual learn to recognize and challenge their thinking patterns and behavior, and to practice these skills outside of the therapeutic sessions during homework tasks.

- Program Flexibility: Some young people, particularly those with ASD, may not be able to access cognitions as readily as others. When this is the case, it is important to adapt the program to the individual's level of understanding. For this reason, it may well be the case that the program will need to place more emphasis on behavioral change than on cognitive change, and in such circumstances this would be entirely appropriate.

For further information about Cognitive Behavior Therapy and its use with young people please refer to Beck (2011) and Stallard (2005).

Adapting CBT for Children with an Autism Spectrum Disorder

Moree and Davis (2010) have provided a good review of the trends in modifying CBT programs that address anxiety for young people with ASD. The predominant trends include

- developing ASD-specific hierarchies;

- using more concrete and visual strategies to explain concepts;

- including the young person's specific interest where possible; and

- engaging actively with parents.

In tailoring an intervention for young people with ASD, it is essential that the program accounts for the cognitive profiles associated with the disorder. This develops capacity to treat target symptoms within a relevant individual context. For example, a revised program may promote social and communication skills alongside strategies that circumvent difficulties with perspective-taking and Theory of Mind. It is also important to adopt a strengths-based approach that celebrates the positive attributes of participants, and allows them to work to their own strengths. In particular, the talents or special interests often identified in individuals with ASD may be used to improve their understanding or, within reason, encourage their motivation.

Specific Features to Be Taken into Account

"Typically developing" young people have an intuitive ability to accurately recognize, name, and describe felt emotions. They also have a similar intuitive ability to interpret or anticipate emotions experienced by others. Ideally, young people develop a wide range of strategies to cope with emotion. Young people with ASD have difficulties with all these abilities (Attwood 2007). Clinical experience and research has demonstrated that many young people with ASD can show deficits in understanding, processing, or describing emotions. With a limited emotional vocabulary, especially for more subtle or complex emotions (Hill, Berthoz, and Frith 2004), young people with ASD can be very "black and white" when talking about their feelings, and it is important to try to extend the range of words available to them. The psychological term "Theory of Mind" refers to the ability to recognize and understand the thoughts and emotions of other people–this is sometimes called "mind reading". There is extensive literature demonstrating that young people with ASD can have difficulties with Theory of Mind. Thus, it is important to be aware that some young people with ASD may struggle to recognize and describe their own inner thoughts and feelings, and so may not be able to tell a parent or teacher when something is distressing. Furthermore, problems with Theory of Mind can cause dysfunctional beliefs and cognitive distortions about the intentions of others. For example, a person with ASD may interpret a benevolent action to have malicious intent, leading to a fear of harm. From a neurotypical perspective, this fear may seem irrational. Though many young people with ASD have good cognitive capacity, they may show cognitive inflexibilities such as a limited range of problem solving strategies, resulting in solutions limited in range, suitability, or efficacy. In turn, this limits their ability to recover from emotional distress. Thus, the affective education and cognitive restructuring components of CBT are particularly important for this population.

Young people with ASD can often show a hyper- or hypo-reactivity to sensory input and sensory experiences. For example, they may experience the noise of a vacuum cleaner, the whirring of a ceiling fan, or the smell of your favorite perfume as aversive and distressing. Specific sensory stimuli may provoke profound anxiety, while the mere prospect of these stimuli in unfamiliar environments may evoke intense negative anticipation. Clinical experience has also identified that young people with ASD are prone to developing perfectionistic tendencies with an almost pathological fear of failure or mistakes. This leads to a tendency to "catastrophize" or "hit the panic button" in situations that others would demonstrate only a relatively mild level of anxiety (Attwood 2007).

While "typically developing" young people are likely to use strategies such as affection, disclosing feelings in a conversation, relaxation, and reflection to alleviate anxiety, those with ASD are less likely to spontaneously access to these strategies. They also have a greater tendency to rely on destruction, solitude, and using a special interest as a means of "thought blocking" to manage anxiety (Attwood and Sofronoff, 2013). Thus, group leaders will need to be aware of young people's relative Theory of Mind abilities, sensory sensitivities, and intense emotional overreactions in the context of a limited repertoire of emotion repair mechanisms.

An individual's unique learning profile must also be recognized and accommodated. Young people with ASD are more responsive to programs that are highly structured and appeal to the logical or scientific thinking associated with ASD. Their cognitive profile can include remarkable visual reasoning abilities, so activities may be enhanced with the use of pictures and drawing and placing less emphasis on conversation (Attwood and Sofronoff 2013). Furthermore, it may take time for the participants to put their strategies into operation as they will, initially, need to be reminded of the link between thought and action.

The Exploring Feelings program is a preventive intervention. It aims to assist young people and parents to develop a ready "toolbox" of techniques they can return to when new situations or challenges arise. The effect of the therapy may not be immediately evident, as both the unique cognitive style and the remitting/relapsing course of anxiety in young people with ASD may obscure early indications of behavioral change.

Involving Parents

There is a mounting wealth of evidence to suggest that involving parents in CBT may produce additional benefits in "typically developing" young people receiving intervention for anxiety symptoms (Dadds, Heard, and Rapee 1992; Barrett, Dadds, and Rapee 1996; and Wood et al. 2006). Programs generally focus on engaging parents to assist their child in acquiring coping skills, and to support the practice of these skills outside of sessions and in anxiety-provoking situations (Wood et al. 2006). This is thought to maximize the impact of the intervention. Studies have shown that a high percentage of parents of "typically developing" young people with anxiety also experience high levels of anxiety themselves (Barrett et al. 1996).

Through active participation in the intervention, parents may derive direct, personal benefit by improving their insight and management of their own anxiety.

There is a long, successful tradition of involving parents of children with autism as "co-therapists" (Schopler and Reichler 1971). This pragmatic approach enhances children's social and communication skills, manages difficult behaviors, and addresses parents' requirements in terms of practical information, education, and advice (McConachie and Diggle 2007). The involvement of parents as co-therapists for these children in middle childhood is much less well-studied. A number of factors may affect the ability of parents to be closely involved. Parents of children with autism are even more stressed than parents of children with other disabilities, and the evidence of higher levels of depression in parents of children with autism is not fully explained by care-giving stress. Some parents feel uncomfortable "playing therapist" and feel it is important to focus on being a parent (McConachie 2003). Nevertheless, the opportunity to learn how to help their child, and to do so in a group setting with other parents to enable mutual support, is one that many parents will welcome.

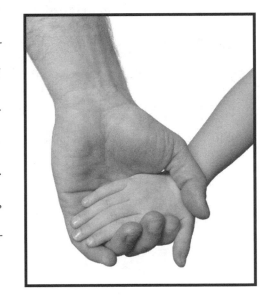

The *Exploring Feelings* workbook describes a randomized, controlled trial in which the group was run involving parents in one of two ways: giving the parents the information as written materials, and teaching the parents all the information in the same manner as the young people (Sofronoff, Attwood, and Hinton 2005). The analysis showed that parents generally regarded the condition in which they were actively trained more positively. In addition, young people in the intervention group combined with parent-trainings showed the greatest improvement in regard to their anxiety symptoms. Involving parents is, therefore, likely to maximize the impact of the intervention, although there are a number of ways in which this can be achieved. These options are discussed further within Section Four.

Offering parents an opportunity to learn the material in a similar manner to the young people is likely to facilitate effective transfer of new skills to the home environment. In addition to learning program content, parents learn and discuss effective techniques to implement new strategies. Within the groups run as part of a UK feasibility pilot evaluation (McConachie et al. 2014), parents described feeling empowered to have a box of tools that they could use with their child in managing anxiety-provoking situations. Some parents also reported experiencing difficulties with anxiety themselves, and described feeling that they could use the same techniques to help to manage their own anxiety.

It may also be helpful to broaden participation within the parents' group by including a grandparent or other relative where both parents are unable to attend. They can provide additional encouragement and support to the young person at home, while supporting the parent attending the group. It is helpful if one of those attending the parents' group attends every session consistently to ensure continuity in relation to the concepts and strategies discussed.

2 Setting Up a Group

Selection of Group Leaders

Exploring Feelings was written in such a way that people without extensive training in CBT would be able to deliver it. However, the program depends on some experience working with young people, running groups, and an understanding of ASD—including its potential impact on group processes. Where group leaders already have some knowledge of CBT, they are likely to be able to adapt to situations flexibly and be creative about how to deliver a particular exercise. It can be a good idea to have a mix of group leaders so that those with complementary skills can be paired.

Training of Group Leaders

Training for group leaders ought to address their needs and skill deficits. In order to tailor training sessions appropriately, it may be helpful to conduct a needs assessment with the individuals selected. It is a good idea to ask the group leaders to read through the Exploring Feelings program and the first section of this manual before they attend training. Helpful components of a group leader training package include

- the characteristics of young people with ASD and the difficulties that may arise when trying to engage them in a group setting;
- the presentation of anxiety in young people with ASD and why levels of anxiety might be so high within this population;
- an overview of the aims of the intervention with detailed focus on the goals, content, and activities for each session;

- the group leaders' expectations and feelings about running the group, highlighting that the young people may find it difficult to grasp some concepts immediately and that it may take longer than anticipated for them to accomplish some aspects of the program;

- thinking through different scenarios, such as how they might handle personal disclosures in the parent or young people's group or challenging behavior; and

- the need to be creative in engaging the young people and parents with the group tasks.

Supervision

Regular supervision is crucial in the running of any group. Supervision can take many forms, but it is helpful to cover a range of topics within each session, including

- a review of the previous group session, focusing on how the participants engaged with the tasks, what worked well, and what was more challenging;

- viewing recorded excerpts of group sessions to highlight strengths and difficulties encountered;

- exploring how the participants interact with one another and the group process;

- sharing ideas about creative ways to explain the concepts or carry out the activities; and

- exploring the content of the next group session to ensure a common understanding of goals and to discuss necessary adjustments for participants' capabilities or group dynamics.

Generally, supervision is most effective if conducted shortly after group sessions—either later that day, or the following morning. This ensures that issues are still fresh in leaders' minds and that they have a chance to "debrief" about the group processes or concerns shortly after the session. In addition, it is helpful to have both the parent and young people's group leaders in supervision together, as this helps to contextualize the experience of each group. For example, some of the issues will be similar across the parent and young people's groups. Information from the parent group can aid thinking about the young person's issues, and how things might be tailored to them.

It is helpful to discuss a range of strategies that group leaders can use in keeping the young people focused and managing challenging behavior, or if individuals become highly distressed. These might include

- having a list of brief games and activities available to break up the session as required;
- revisiting ground rules set by the group;
- working one-on-one with an individual; or
- tailoring rewards and tasks to an individual's special interests.

In addition, it is important to have an extra member of staff around to offer support in taking an individual for time out, or to step into the group while the group leader takes the individual for a short time to calm down or talk about their difficulties. There does need to be an explicit procedure in place for managing difficulties that arise with either a child or a parent, as well as a clear protocol for referral to additional services (e.g., signpost families to the child and adolescent mental health services).

Quality of Program Delivery

In order to achieve the expected outcomes, it is important that the program is delivered essentially as it was intended. Having group leaders complete a checklist at the end of each session helps to counteract drift-away from scheduled content. It also aids reflection on what happened in the session and can be referred to during supervision. As part of the UK feasibility pilot trial of Exploring Feelings (McConachie et al. 2014), fidelity checklists were developed, listing all of the activities to complete within each session so that the group leaders could check whether they were meeting all the components of the group (i.e., both content and CBT style of delivery). The fidelity checklists are shown in Appendix 1.

Inviting the Young People

Who to Invite

When running a group, it is important to consider its composition—not only in terms of size, but also in terms of the characteristics of the young people involved. It is useful to gather detailed information about each child before deciding whether to include them in a group. It may be important to consider a wide range of characteristics such as age, maturity, gender, intellectual ability, interests, and any additional needs (such as sensitivity to noise) that may need to be accommodated. It is also important to consider some of the potential group dynamics that may result: only having one girl in a group, for example, or running a group with a wide age range.

Having said that, there will be young people who are not yet ready for the program, and certain behavioral difficulties should be managed before a program such as this is offered. For those young people who present with significant Attention Deficit Hyperactivity Disorder (ADHD) features and take medication to attend school, it may be helpful to ask that they also take medication to attend the group. It may also be a good idea to try to ensure that there is only one young person with ADHD in a group, so that this can be managed as effectively as possible.

There may be young people for whom such a group is unsuitable because they may struggle to integrate, or because their behavior may jeopardize the success of the group. This might include young people

with significant oppositional behavior who may steer the group away from its function, or young people with unmanaged ADHD who may find it difficult to keep their focus and attention on the task at hand during the two-hour sessions. In these cases, it is likely to be important to refer the parents for additional help in managing the young person's behavior before they are invited to participate in a group. It is also important to consider the young person's readiness to participate in the group—perhaps by exploring their emotional understanding and engaging in some preparatory work before inviting them. Programs such as Whiz Kids (www.autismgames.com.au) or Transporters (www.thetransporters.com), for instance, increase emotional awareness and enable them to more successfully engage with the concepts and strategies discussed in the group.

How to Invite Young People

One important aspect of running a group is thinking about how to share information about the program with the young people to best engage them in the collaborative process. It is crucial for the organizers and group leaders to meet with the families beforehand to explain the group process and answer any questions they may have. It is important to raise with parents that the terms "autism" or "Autism Spectrum Disorder" may be used in the sessions, so that they are aware of this and can discuss it with their child if needed. In addition, to reduce the young people's anxieties and increase their familiarity with the program, it might be helpful to develop an illustrated leaflet that tells them about what to expect and introduces the group leaders. An example of a leaflet explaining the group is shown in Appendix 2.

Following the running of Exploring Feelings as part of a pilot evaluation study (McConachie et al. 2014), a DVD was developed which captures the experiences of some of the families taking part. Such a resource could be shown to prospective participants so they can hear the views of those who have already been through the intervention. It is hoped that this may increase their understanding of what the Exploring Feelings group entails, and reduce their anxieties about taking part.

If you decide to make a similar DVD, below are some interview questions you might use. They reflect the kind of information families often ask about at first when approached about participating.

- Did you enjoy the Exploring Feelings group?

- How many other children were there? How many parents? Was that about right?

- What kinds of things do you do in the group?

- What were the best things or what did you feel was most helpful to you?

- What happens if someone gets scared or anxious or annoyed in the group?

- Was the project work useful? Did you work on it together?

- Have you used the techniques you learned since the group ended?

When to Run Groups

The schedule for group sessions should aim to maximize attendance and engagement. There are obviously a great number of factors impacting a family's attendance at a group including school, work commitments, extra-curricular activities, mealtimes, bedtimes, and the potential presence of other siblings at home. The Exploring Feelings group has been run on weekends (Sofronoff et al. 2005) and during weekday evenings (McConachie et al. 2014), both of which have their benefits and drawbacks. It is also important to consider the timing of the group in relation to the school holidays to prevent, if possible, the need for a break in the group session. Young people may find it difficult to settle back into group after a break, impacting on the success of the session immediately after the holiday.

Who Needs to Be There

It is ideal to have two group leaders available to run an Exploring Feelings group for young people, with a third group leader dedicated to the parent group. As mentioned above, in our experience it was helpful to have an additional member of staff around as a reserve assistant or as a stand-in when needed. This member of staff was there to greet the families as they arrived and check how everyone was doing, allowing the group leaders time to set up the equipment needed for the session. They also provided additional support in the event of a participant's distress or challenging behavior by taking the participant for time-out, or by replacing the group leader who could then focus on resolving any difficulties.

A Suitable Venue

Another important aspect of setting up a group is finding a suitable venue. Parents and young people's feedback was that it was ideal for this to be at a community site rather than at a clinic or hospital site. It was helpful to have two large group rooms, as well as a spare room to be used as a waiting room when the families arrived, for breaks between sessions, or as a time-out room if needed. It was also important to think about the

location of the venue, ensuring that it has good public transport links and is easily accessible for the people you are intending to invite to the group.

Equipment

In order to run the group, you will need a number of items for each of the activities. A checklist of items needed throughout the program is shown in Appendix 3. In addition, you will also need to develop hand-outs for both the young people and their parents to record the important information discussed within each of the sessions. An example of a handout produced for each of the young people's sessions is shown in Appendices 4-8. The agenda for each session is written up on a piece of flip chart paper beforehand, so that the young people and parents have a visual reminder of what the session will cover and what is coming next.

Parent Group

The tasks and activities in the young people's group focus on their personal experiences. The parent group uses the initial sessions to work through the materials from their own perspective, and to gain insight into what their children are doing. The group leaders may find it useful to work flexibly between examples that parents provide of their own anxiety alongside those of their children. Indeed, parents may spontaneously alternate between the two, and may find the opportunity to reflect on and consider strategies to manage their own anxiety helpful.

Follow-Up

It may be helpful to consider offering a "top-up" group session to both parents and young people, or just parents. This would enable them to try out the strategies discussed in the group, and then come back together for a session to reflect on what they have found helpful and explore any strategies or situations that they are finding more challenging. It is likely to be helpful to have this session no less than three months after the last session, to give the group time to consolidate their knowledge of the strategies discussed and have ample time to try these out within their daily lives.

Evaluation

Since the aim of the program is to help with the young person's anxiety, it is useful to use a measure of anxiety before starting the program, after it is finished, and again at the follow-up session. It is a good idea to use both a measure of anxiety completed by the young person and a measure completed by the parent. Some measures that have been used include

- The Spence Children's Anxiety Scale (SCAS; Spence 1998);
- The Spence Children's Anxiety Scale – Parent version (SCAS-P; Nauta et al. 2004); and
- Anxiety Disorders Interview Schedule (ADIS) parent report (Silverman and Albano 1996).

It may also be relevant to use a measure of child behavior. This could be the case in a school setting where it may be felt that anxiety is having an impact on a child's behavior. Some measures that could be used include

- The Strengths and Difficulties Questionnaire (Goodman 1997);
- The Eyberg Child behavior Checklist (Eyberg and Eyberg 1998); and
- The Conner's Rating Scale (Conners 1997).

In addition, the *Exploring Feelings* manual includes a specific outcome measure called "James and the Math Test," which is designed to evaluate whether each young person has understood the concepts and strategies presented through the program. The young person reads the scenario and then has to generate possible strategies to manage the situation. The scenario is one that is typically anxiety-provoking for a young person with ASD, and at the beginning of the intervention we would expect that many young people would have few effective strategies. One of the aims of the program is to try to increase the number of strategies each young person has in his or her repertoire. Since this scenario will be presented to the young person on more than one occasion, it is important to acknowledge that they have given answers before and that we want to know if they can recall the good suggestions that they had last time, and whether they have any to add. If this is not explained, then some young people will simply not give the responses that they have offered previously, and you will not have a good illustration of what they have learned.

We suggest that for many young people, it will be best for the scenario to be read aloud and for the responses to be written down by the group leader. This means that handwriting can be deciphered more easily, and anything that is unclear can be clarified with the young person immediately. It is okay to ask, "What do you mean by that?" (e.g., if the young person suggests something vague such as "Be brave"). What we then have is the best that the young person can do on this particular occasion.

In terms of scoring "James and the Math Test," we suggest the following guidelines:

- Award one point for each appropriate response, and zero points for each inappropriate or unhelpful response.

- For a strategy to be scored as one point, it must be appropriate to the situation (i.e., the classroom). While "taking a shower to cool down" may be okay at home, this will not work at school. Parents are also not likely to be at school.

- Score separate points for responses that are related but not exactly the same (e.g., slow breathing and counting slowly and squeezing a stress ball). These are all relaxation strategies but, each one is different. This is the same for different thinking strategies.

- Score one point for thinking positively, and then additional points for each example of positive/ helpful thoughts (e.g., "think positive" or "I can do this if I focus" each earn one point).

- Imagining good things (e.g., "think about something I like") is scored separately from helpful thoughts.

- Do not score repetitions of strategies, even if the words are different.

ONE POINT EXAMPLES	ZERO POINT EXAMPLES
Get to know the teacher	"Just be quiet" (not a specific strategy)
Tell the teacher they get anxious	"Just stay calm" (not a specific strategy)
Ask the teacher or a friend for help	Ask a friend for help on the test
Study/revise for test if there is time	Suggestions for how to do sums (in their head, etc.)
Trying hard on the test/focus on the test	Responses inappropriate to the situation/location
Go slowly on the test/try easy problems first	Repetitions of strategies

3 Possible Adaptations to the Core Program

As part of the UK based pilot RCT of Exploring Feelings (McConachie et al. 2014), a number of modifications were made to the original program. These are detailed in the following section on a session-by-session basis.

Getting to Know You Session

Given the severity of the young people's anxiety, it may be important to spend additional time allowing the young people taking part in the group to get to know each other and "form" as a group. The number of tasks to complete within session one is quite high, therefore you may want to consider adding an additional session at the start of the program, making it seven sessions in total. This additional session should last two hours and focus on introducing the young people to each other and the group leaders, setting ground rules for the group, and completing some of the "Getting to Know You" activities from session one (i.e., "My Favorite," "Strengths and Talents," "What's Good About Me," and "Special Interests").

Ground rules are a crucial aspect to running any group, therefore, it is helpful to ask the young people to generate some rules that will be important to the group. These should be phrased positively in terms of behaviors, such as "listening when others are talking." It also may be helpful to complete a brief "Getting to Know You" activity as part of the first session to reduce anxiety around the group situation, such as passing a ball to one another, with child receiving the ball telling the group a fact about him or herself.

At the end of the initial "Getting to Know You" session, some project work can be introduced to begin the process of engaging the young people in the collaborative nature of the group. For the first project, you may wish to offer the group the choice of completing the "Things to be Happy About" task, or the "Happiness Diary." Although this means that these tasks would be completed before the feeling of happiness has been explored within Session One, the early introduction of project work might provide a useful prompt for the young people to explore the feeling of happiness in the next week.

Session One

We ran this session in line with the workbook, starting with a review of the project work and then moving onto the "Being Happy" activities. However, we made a couple of changes. We took out both of the rope games involving grading words to describe happy or relaxed, as we felt this was quite challenging for the young people. Instead, we asked them to generate their own words that they used to describe feeling happy or relaxed. This allowed more time to focus on the central aspects of the session, such as recognizing when they felt happy or relaxed, and practicing relaxation techniques. See Appendix 9 for a copy of the relaxation scripts used. We felt that the relaxation techniques were so valuable to the young people that we made time at the end of each session to practice one, giving the young people the option of which relaxation approach was used.

For the project work, we chose to focus on one activity. The young people created cue cards of pictures that made them feel relaxed, which they could keep with them at all times. We chose not to ask the young people to complete the questionnaire about feeling anxious as this had already been completed prior to the start of the group.

Session Two

In this session, we spent additional time ensuring that the young people had a clear understanding of what anxiety meant. We discussed which words participants used to describe anxiety, so that we developed a shared language to discuss the issues. The only adaptation we made to this section was to take out the "heroes that become anxious" task, as this did not seem particularly relevant for the young people and allowed for more time to focus on the other tasks.

Session Three

In order to fit with the participants' understanding, we renamed "inappropriate tools" as "unhelpful tools."

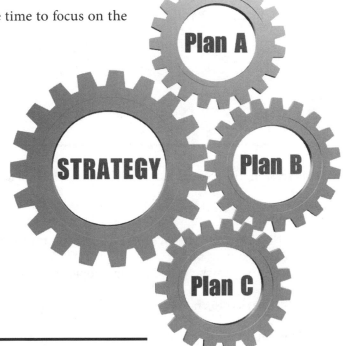

Session Four

We chose to focus the majority of this session on the "Anxiety Hierarchy" task

from the project work, as we felt that this was central to the intervention. Interestingly, we found that the young people often needed a significant level of support in completing this task, and so undertaking it within the main group rather than at home seemed to be beneficial as group leaders could be of assistance. We gave each person a sheet of flip chart paper and post-it notes and asked them to write down things that made them feel anxious, and then stick them against the thermometer in terms of how anxious they made them feel. Group leaders moved between the young people, providing support and helping to rank relative levels of anxiety. We collected the thermometers at the end of the group so that we could transfer the ideas onto a handout to take home. For homework, we helped the young people select one or two anxiety-provoking situations from the hierarchy to practice their toolbox on, making sure that they chose some of their lower-end anxieties to increase the likelihood of some immediate success. We also provided a diary sheet to accompany the project work task, so that the young people could easily record their use of tools and how successful they found them (see Appendix 10). When completing these exercises, it is a good idea to also remind young people how they know when they are starting to feel less anxious (i.e., what happens to your body? Your heart rate? Your thoughts?). By focusing on the sensation of reducing anxiety, the child is more likely to stick with a strategy for a little while to check if it is working.

Session Five

In this session, the "Social Story" task was completed as a group on the flip chart using a comic strip style approach. We asked the young people to choose an anxious situation to write the social story on (see Appendix 11 for an example). We gave each group member a chance to lead the suggestions for what should go in each box, but the other young people could add their suggestions too. In terms of generating the thoughts, we tried to encourage each of the young people to generate one.

We adapted the "Antidote to Poisonous Thoughts" task so that it was more recognizable to our audience by using the terms "unhelpful" or "helpful" thoughts. However, the Friends Program (Barrett, Webster & Turner, 1999) refers to these types of thoughts as "red" and "green" thoughts, and this could be another way to help the young people understand the concept. Instead of completing this as an individual task, we completed it as a group activity. Each of the statements was written on a card, and each person took it in turns to decide whether it was a helpful or unhelpful thought, then placed it under the right heading on the floor. This allowed for discussion around how the young people had reached their decisions, and a chance to correct any misinterpretations.

We also completed the "Creating Antidotes to Poisonous Thoughts" task as a group exercise. Each person generated an antidote on the flip chart using the items given in the manual (altered to fit the audience), and some related to the concerns of participants gathered from the earlier sessions or the completed anxiety questionnaires (SCAS).

For the project work, we gave the young people and parents an example of the social story, using the same format as used in the session, as a template to use if they wanted and an example about experiencing anxiety (see Appendix 12). We tried to encourage as much creativity as possible in how the young people generated the social story. In one of the groups, for example, the young person was a keen photographer. He chose to take photos of himself and his mother in various situations, and then added speech bubbles to these to show what was going on. To promote challenging unhelpful thoughts by replacing them with more helpful thoughts, we gave the young people a record sheet with the headings side-by-side to help them to visualize the process (see Appendix 13).

Session Six

In the final session, we completed the "sharing strategies" task as a group exercise, selecting an anxiety-provoking situation that was relevant to the group members and working through it using all the strategies covered throughout the program.

We also included an evaluation element for both the young people and parents. In the young people's group, we asked a number of questions to evaluate the success of the group, including:

- If you were to describe the group using one word, which word would you choose?
- If you were to pick an animal to describe the group, which one would you choose and why?
- How could we improve the group if we were to run it again in the future?
- What have you enjoyed most about the group? What was your favorite session/task and why?
- What have you least enjoyed about the group? What was your least favorite session/task and why?

We asked the parents to complete an evaluation questionnaire, a copy of which can be found in Appendix 14. We also asked the group the following questions:

- What was most helpful about the group?
- What was least helpful about the group?
- How could we improve the group if we were to run it again in the future?

At the end of the final session we gave out certificates to both the parent and young people, either within the individual groups or together as a larger group.

4 Different Settings For Groups

This section will focus on the different settings in which the Exploring Feelings group has been run, and the resulting differences in the group setup and structure in these environments. These include running the group within an Australian Metropolitan University setting, a UK Child and Adolescent Mental Health Service (CAMHS), a mainstream school, and a specialist school setting.

University Clinic Research Trial

The Exploring Feelings program has been run on four occasions through the psychology clinic at the University of Queensland, Australia. In the original trial, seventy-two young people were randomly assigned to one of three conditions: a group in which the young people received the program and parents were given the materials and asked to help their child with the home tasks, a treatment-as-usual group, and a group in which both young people and parents completed the same material in the six two-hour sessions. The program was run by intern psychologists completing their training in the psychology clinic. Groups were held on a Saturday, and interns were supervised in small groups. We found that more parents (especially fathers) were able to attend on Saturdays, and young people did not need to miss school or arrive tired after a stressful day. The drawback to weekends is that some young people may participate in other activities, and family commitments need to be taken into account.

The major focus of this trial was to evaluate the efficacy of the program, but we were also interested to know whether there was an additional benefit of training parents rigorously in the program. We were also keen to know whether the program was acceptable to both parents and young people. We found the parents reported that they gained great benefit from the large parent group, beyond the acquisition of knowledge and strategies. Parents spoke about feeling able to speak openly about the issues and concerns that they had for their children, because they quickly learned that the other parents were having similar experiences. They spoke about developing a shared language with their child that allowed them to better understand their child's perspective, and to become more confident in their ability to help their child manage anxiety-provoking situations. In some cases, the young people formed friendships and the parents formed support groups. Most of these outcomes were not anticipated and not measured in a quantitative way. Some skill is required in managing a large parent group to ensure that the material is covered so that everyone can understand and use it, and to ensure that a few parents do not overtake the group with individual concerns and questions. It can also be useful to actively complete exercises rather than rely on verbal explanations; this allows a demonstration that parents do understand, and accommodates parents who may themselves have traits of ASD and benefit from a more concrete approach.

The sessions with the young people were an evolving process. Each group was made up of three young people and two interns. This allowed for flexibility within the groups and for some one-to-one time for each young person as required. It also meant that any behavior issues could be managed; a young person could take a break if needed, and any young person who did not want to write could be accommodated. We found that the sessions functioned best if the content was broken up with games, rewards (stickers worked well), and when the focus was positive for each young person (i.e., the quiet young person rewarded for offering an answer, the talkative young person rewarded for listening, and so on). Ground rules were established by the young people in session one and were phrased positively. A reminder could take the form of asking: "What should be done when someone else is talking?", and then the young person could be praised and rewarded for remembering and complying. Young people were assigned to groups based on age and gender. This meant that stickers and prizes could be gender specific. We also tried to accommodate special interests in the reward system whenever possible.

Parent-Delivered Program

A second trial of the program was conducted in which parents were trained to deliver the content to their own child at home. Parents were trained in two half-day workshops on consecutive Saturdays. Following this, they received weekly phone consults from an intern psychologist to track how they were doing, discuss any problems, and brainstorm difficulties. The results from this trial were quite promising; they were slightly better than the young person-only condition of the original trial, and parents reported a more immediate decrease in child anxiety than in the original trial. There are two possible explanations for this. One explanation is that the effect was more immediate because the parents were applying the strategies more consistently and in the environment in which the anxiety occurred. A second explanation is that the parents had a greater investment in the success of the program and there was a halo effect.

Parents did also report qualitative changes similar to the original trial. We felt the use of two training occasions was useful because parents who had questions after the first workshop could ask them in the group, and everyone would benefit. It also allowed for the parents to meet and share their experiences in a way similar to the original trial.

University Clinic Fee-Based Delivery

We have offered the program twice since the original trials through the university clinic on a fee-for-service basis. We still retain the same format of three young people, two interns, and a large parent group. We have always used an amount from the fee to purchase stickers and small prizes for the young people as well as tea, coffee, and cookies for the parents, and pizza and certificates for the follow-up session. Over the years, we have also placed an increasing emphasis on the importance of parent engagement. We ask parents each week to describe instances of when they have encouraged their child to use strategies, and when the young person has actually used them. Interns meet with parents for about five minutes before each session to check what has been done at home, and briefly again at the end of the session to let parents know how the young person did in session—what they did well (always focus on the positive), and what they might need to practice more. While we have not collected data on home practice and parent involvement, anecdotally, we would suggest that this is the best predictor of child outcome.

UK Child and Adolescent Mental Health Service (CAMHS)

By definition, young people seen within CAMHS are presenting with mental health problems that are significantly impacting their daily lives. Given that CAMH Services have limited resources, it can be seen as more time-efficient and cost-effective to offer a group intervention to those experiencing similar difficulties. Furthermore, being part of a group can offer additional benefits, including meeting others with similar difficulties, developing new skills in interacting with others, and providing emotional support.

When setting up a group within CAMHS, careful consideration needs to be taken in terms of who to include in the group and the potential group dynamics. A number of young people attending CAMHS present with co-morbid difficulties, which need to be considered when deciding whether they would be suitable for a particular group. For example, children who also have Attention Deficit Hyperactivity Disorder (ADHD) may have difficulties staying focused on a task, and this may impact on the group's progress.

The groups were run on a weekday evening and lasted two hours. The decision was made to run the groups from five to seven o'clock in the evening to avoid school and typical work hours. There were four to five young people in a group, and their respective parents or other relatives in the parents group, with this generally comprising up to ten people. The groups were run at a community site rather than an NHS or hospital site, which the participants reported finding more accessible.

The groups were run by Trainee Clinical Psychologists, Assistant Psychologists, Community CAMHS Nurses, and Clinical Psychologists. Supervision was provided on a weekly basis by Clinical Psychologists with a special interest in ASD.

In setting up the groups, we decided to structure the sessions so that the majority of the tasks were completed as a group rather than individually. Afterward, we would get together to share ideas. We felt that this increased the young people's experience of a group, provided greater opportunities for interaction and socializing, and also enhanced the potential solutions and ideas generated. In addition, a number of the young people taking part in these groups had difficulties with reading and writing, and so this structure minimized the impact of these difficulties. However, each group is adapted to suit the needs of the participating individuals; it may be beneficial for some groups to complete the tasks more individually if this is their preference, or if individualized attention is needed in order to manage behavior or complete the tasks. The parents' group was run in exactly the same way as the young people's group and covered all the same material. Parents supported the young people in completing their project work rather than completing the activities for themselves.

In order to help the young people and parents focus on each of the sessions in turn, we put the workbooks into a loose-leaf folder for each person and the handout for each session was given out as the group went along, so as not to overwhelm the group or allow them to race ahead.

Mainstream School Setting

An Exploring Feelings group was run in a mainstream primary school setting with seven young people. All but one had a diagnosis of ASD, and in this case there was evidence to suggest that the young person had ASD characteristics without a confirmed diagnosis. Ages ranged from nine to eleven and the group included one girl. The group was facilitated by two Local Authority Specialist Senior Educational Psychologists and a Teaching Assistant from the school.

The process involved a meeting with senior school staff to explain the project, identify group participants, identify the member of staff who would be released to support the group, and agree to their role in supporting the group throughout the school week. This included time to informally mentor the young people and to encourage the practice and generalization of specific strategies.

A meeting also took place with the parents, who were given information about the Exploring Feelings central themes. They were encouraged to participate in and support "homework" activities, which contributed to each young person's folder that was built up week by week.

The central themes of the Exploring Feelings program were followed, but activities were adapted to support different learning styles with a greater emphasis on active and practical activities.

Many of the young people in the group were reluctant to record activities using a pen and paper, but were more confident and enthusiastic in using the Interactive Whiteboard. They chose to record their ideas using drawings, text, and clipart. Access to the whiteboard and printing facilities appeared to play to personal strengths and preferences, which increased group participation.

Each young person made a personal keyring of positive images, which they were allowed to use in school.

Guided imagery relaxation scripts and music were used to help the young people explore relaxation, and were both effective and popular. This activity was repeated in different sessions.

An advantage in running the group within a mainstream setting was the access to a teaching assistant who joined each session. She was able share information with other members of school staff and to act as a mentor to support and encourage the practice of different strategies and emotional tools. She also provided feedback as to how the young people had coped in school between sessions. A further advantage was the direct access to facilities and the minimization of time spent traveling or out of mainstream lessons.

Issues for consideration in running a group in a mainstream setting include

- the need for effective liaison with senior staff in school to ensure understanding and ongoing support once the program has finished;

- the involvement of an identified school staff member who can support the long-term practice of strategies;

- the possible impact of timings for sessions in relation to the school day and school week;

- the planning of sessions in relation to school holidays (it may not be possible to run all sessions without a break for school holidays); and

- the possible impact of other activities in school which might affect the planned program (e.g., school trips, project weeks, etc.).

Specialist School Setting

Two Exploring Feelings groups were run in a special needs school, with four or five young people in each group. The young people were grouped as closely as possible by age, and all had a similar level of cognitive function. The school was a specialist school for young people with a primary diagnosis of language disorder. Many of the young people also had a diagnosis of ASD, with a further sub-set where a diagnosis had not been officially made, but medical records indicated possible ASD features. The group format described previously was adhered to, with only minor adaptations, such as using post-it notes on a wall rather than a rope for the "rope" game.

The group was run by a clinical psychologist who specializes in autism and related disorders, a teacher from the school, and a trainee clinical psychologist. It was run during the school day, which required the young people to miss a lesson each week. One difficulty was that the teachers whose lessons were missed, while they acknowledged the value and need for the group, expressed some disappointment at having to release young people for six consecutive lessons. Another difficulty was that running a parent group was not an option, as many of the pupils came to the school from far and wide via taxi rather than parental pick up and drop off.

None of the young people presented with behavioral difficulties, but many had difficulty maintaining focus. An advantage of keeping numbers small meant there were enough adults to give the young people individual support when required.

One advantage of running groups within a special needs setting was recruitment; as anxiety problems occur at a much higher prevalence than in the mainstream setting, teachers had no difficulty identifying a number of eligible participants. This also made selecting participants on the basis of age and ability relatively straightforward, as there was a large selection pool. Having a teacher familiar with the children's special needs co-run the group was a distinct advantage. Having a co-leader who was on-site was also extremely useful for logistics; for example, if a participant was late for the group, they were quickly located and able to use follow-up measures.

Another advantage of running the group in a special needs setting was the availability of equipment to suit the young people's needs. For example, Swiss balls or other adapted seats for those children who had difficulty sitting still, or adapted pens or sloping desks for those with writing difficulties proved helpful.

Both quantitative and qualitative outcomes were obtained. Quantitative measures included the Beck Youth Inventory (Beck, Beck, & Jolly 2005) and the Strengths and Difficulties Questionnaire. Qualitative outcomes included an informal questionnaire asking teachers and parents whether they had noticed any difference in the participant's anxiety, whether they noticed them using any of the strategies, and any general comments for improving the group.

In keeping with the philosophy of the program, a highly visual method was employed when delivering the group. All worksheets and material generated as part of the groups collated at the end into a folder, which the participants could keep. Parents and staff were informed about this folder and asked to encourage the participants to refer back to the folders as often as possible.

References

Attwood, T. 2004. *Exploring Feelings: Anxiety. Cognitive Behavior Therapy to Manage Anxiety.* Arlington: Future Horizons.

_____. 2007. *The Complete Guide to Asperger's Syndrome.* London: Jessica Kingsley Publishers.

Attwood, T., and K. Sofronoff. 2013. Prevention of Anxiety in Children and Adolescents with Autism and Asperger Syndrome, in *The Wiley-Blackwell Handbook of The Treatment of Childhood and Adolescent Anxiety* (eds C. A. Essau and T. H. Ollendick). Chichester, West Sussex, UK: John Wiley & Sons, Ltd.

Barrett, P.M., M.R. Dadds, and R.M. Rapee. 1996. "Family Treatment of Childhood Anxiety: A Controlled Trial." *Journal of Consulting and Clinical Psychology* 64: 333-342.

Barrett, P.M., M.R. Dadds, R.M. Rapee, and S. Ryan. 1996. "Family Enhancement of Cognitive Styles in Anxious and Aggressive Children." *Journal of Abnormal Child Psychology* 24: 187-203.

Beaumont, R., and K. Sofronoff. 2008. "A Multi-Component Social Skills Intervention for Children with Asperger Syndrome: The Junior Detective Training Program." *Journal of Child Psychology and Psychiatry* 49 (7): 743-753.

Beck, J.S. 2011. *Cognitive Behavior Therapy: Basics and Beyond* (Second Edition). New York: Guilford Press.

Dadds, M.R., P.M. Heard, and R.M. Rapee. 1992. "The Role of Family Intervention in the Treatment of Child Anxiety Disorders: Some Preliminary Findings." *Behavior Change* 9: 171-177.

de Bruin, E.L., R.F. Ferdinand, S. Meester, F.A. de Nijs, and F. Verheij. 2007. "High Rates of Psychiatric Co-Morbidity in PDD-NOS." *Journal of Autism and Developmental Disorders* 37: 877-886.

Gadow, K.D., J. Roohi, C.J. DeVincent, S. Kirsch, and E. Hatchwell. 2010. "Brief Report: Glutamate Transporter Gene (SLC1A1) Single Nucleotide Polymorphism (rs301430) and Repetitive Behaviors and Anxiety in Children with Autism Spectrum Disorder." *Journal of Autism and Developmental Disorders* 40: 1139-1145.

Ghaziuddin, M. 2002. "Asperger Syndrome: Associated Psychiatric and Medical Conditions." *Focus on Autism and Other Developmental Disabilities* 17(3): 138-144

Goodman, R. 1997. "The Strengths and Difficulties Questionnaire: A Research Note." *Journal of Child Psychology and Psychiatry* 38: 581-586

Guttman-Steinmetz, S., K.D. Gadow, C.J. De Vincent, and J. Crowell. 2010. "Anxiety Symptoms in Boys with Autism Spectrum Disorder, aAtention-Deficit Hyperactivity Disorder, or Chronic Multiple Tic Disorder and Community Controls." *Journal of Autism and Developmental Disorders* 40: 1006-1016.

Hill, E., S. Berthoz, And U. Frith. 2004. "Cognitive Processing of Own Emotions in Individuals with Autistic Spectrum Disorder and in Their Relatives." *Journal of Autism and Developmental Disorders* 34: 229-235.

Joosten, A.V., A.C. Bundy, and S.L. Einfeld. 2009. "Intrinsic and Extrinsic Motivation for Stereotypic and Repetitive Behavior." *Journal of Autism and Developmental Disorders* 39: 521-531.

McConachie, H. 2003. "Intervention with Parents of Young Children with Asperger Syndrome." In W Yule (ed) Interventions for Individuals with Asperger's Syndrome. Occasional Paper No 21. London: Association of Child Psychology and Psychiatry, pp 33-37.

McConachie, H., and T. Diggle. 2007. "Parent-Implemented Early Intervention for Young Children with Autism Spectrum Disorder: A Systematic Review." *Journal of Evaluation in Clinical Practice* 13 (1): 120-129.

McConachie, H., M. Freeston, V. Grahame, C. Hemm, E. Honey, A. Le Couteur, E. McLaughlin, J. Rodgers, N. Steen, L. Tavernor, and H. Taylor. 2014. "Group Therapy for Anxiety in Children with Autism Spectrum Disorder." *Autism* 18 (6): 723 - 732.

Moree, B.N., and T.E. Davis. 2010. "Cognitive-Behavioral Therapy for Anxiety in Children Diagnosed with Autism Spectrum Disorders: Modification Trends." *Research in Autism Spectrum Disorders* 4: 346-354.

Schopler, E., and R. Reichler. 1971. "Parents as Co-Therapists in the Treatment of Psychotic Children." *Journal of Autism and Childhood Schizophrenia* 1 (1): 87–102

Sofronoff, K., T. Attwood, and S. Hinton. 2005. "A Randomised Control Trial of a CBT Intervention for Anxiety in Children with Asperger Syndrome." *Journal of Child Psychology and Psychiatry* 46: 1152-1160.

Sofronoff, K., E. Dark, and V. Stone. 2011. "Social Vulnerability and Bullying in Children with Asperger Syndrome." *Autism* 15 (3): 355-372.

Stallard, P. 2005. *A Clinician's Guide to Think Good, Feel Good: Using CBT with Children and Young People.* Wiley-Blackwell.

Van Steensel, F.J.A., S.M. Bogels, and S. Perrin. 2011. "Anxiety Disorders in Children and Adolescents with Autistic Spectrum Disorders: A Meta-Analysis." *Clinical Child and Family Psychology Review* 14: 302-317.

Wood, J.J., and K.D. Gadow. 2010. "Exploring the Nature and Function of Anxiety in Youth with Autism Spectrum Disorders." *Clinical Psychology: Science and Practice* 17 (4): 281-292.

Wood, J.J., B.C. Chu J.C. Piacentini, M. Sigman, and M. Southam-Gerow. 2006. "Family Cognitive Behavioral Therapy for Child Anxiety Disorders." *Journal of the American Academy of Child and Adolescent Psychiatry* 45 (3): 314-321

Date: _____

Group Leader: _____

Session Number/Title: _____

Number of Participants: _____

PLEASE INDICATE WHICH OF THE FOLLOWING COMPONENTS WERE COMPLETED IN YOUR GROUP:

CBT components	Present	To what extent was this used (please circle)
Session Structure	Yes or No	0 = not at all 1 = briefly covered but insufficiently 2 = covered adequately 3 = comprehensively covered
1. An agenda was set (including nature and timing of sessions and the schedule of contacts).		0 1 2 3
2. Participants were invited to add to the agenda.		0 1 2 3
3. Previous session was summarized.		0 1 2 3
4. Homework/project work was reviewed.		0 1 2 3
5. This session was summarized at the end.		0 1 2 3
6. Homework was set and any questions answered.		0 1 2 3
7. End of session feedback was elicited.		0 1 2 3
Techniques used during session	Yes or No	0 = not at all 1 = minimal evidence 2 = several examples 3 = consistently
8. Collaborative approach i.e., group leaders work with participants to consider how best to use strategies, problem solve in relation to any difficulties experienced, and allow participant to express concerns or query material. (N.B., some session content requires facilitators to present a lot of information, the key element is the extent to which information is presented as hypotheses to consider/ reflect upon rather than as facts—relative to the participants ability level).		0 1 2 3

9. Non-blaming attitudes i.e., group leaders demonstrate empathy and understanding of the participants position and praise them whenever appropriate.		0	1	2	3
Techniques used during session		0	1	2	3
10. Individualizes the therapy for participants i.e., group leaders explicitly personalize the general information to relate to child/family. Group leaders encourage reflection on how the information relates to the participant. Group leaders reflect upon previous information provided by participants to illustrate concepts.	Individualizes the therapy for participants	0	1	2	3
11. Explores the link between thoughts, feelings, and behavior—including orientation to the model i.e., help individuals identify thoughts, feelings and behaviors associated with specific situations, but also the links between these factors.		0	1	2	3
12. Skills/strategy development i.e., helps participants to develop skills/strategies to manage anxiety. These can be behavioral (e.g., breathing/PMR) or cognitive (e.g., thought challenging).		0	1	2	3
13. Exposure/desensitization i.e., uses exposure therapy with participants in relation to their specific anxieties. Includes introduction of the concept, planning, and implementation of exposure and review.	Explores the link between thoughts, feelings, and behavior—including orientation to the model	0	1	2	3
14. Relapse prevention i.e., helps participants to consolidate skills/strategies used and plan for use in new anxiety-provoking situations.		0	1	2	3

Generic acceptable therapeutic components	0 = not at all 1 = minimal evidence 2 = several examples 3 = consistently

15. Group leaders foster good therapeutic alliance with group participants. i.e., develop an empathic, warm, and genuine relationship.	0	1	2	3
16. Group leaders communicate effectively using appropriate empathic statements, reflections, clarification, verbal, and non-verbal behaviors.	0	1	2	3
17. Group leaders seek feedback from participants.	0	1	2	3
18. Emotional content of sessions managed. i.e., a safe space is created.	0	1	2	3
19. Difficult behaviors are managed appropriately i.e., time-out may be necessary.	0	1	2	3

Unacceptable Non-CBT components	0 = not at all 1 = minimal evidence 2 = several examples 3 = consistently			
20. Unstructured play therapy i.e., allowing participants the freedom to select and engage in unstructured and undirected activities without an identified objective.	0	1	2	3
21. Use of interpretations of behaviors or comments i.e., commenting on a person's unconscious motivation for making a comment or behaving in a particular way.	0	1	2	3
22. Use of externalization techniques i.e., referring to anxiety as something external to the participant (e.g., "what does anxiety look like?").	0	1	2	3
23. Use of a purely didactive approach Didactic is defined by the lack of any opportunity for discussion, reflection, and consideration of how information applies to the participants in the group.	0	1	2	3
24. Presents information in abstract/general form with no reference to or questions about how it applies to the participant.	0	1	2	3
25. Unnecessary deviation from the session topic/irrelevant content covered.	0	1	2	3
26. Other: Please describe	0	1	2	3

Exploring Feelings Group

On (date) I will be starting the Exploring Feelings group at (location). At the group I will learn things that will help me to understand feelings better, and manage anxious feelings better.

At the group I will meet other young people like me. They will also learn how to understand feelings better.

We will do different activities together, like drawing and role-play.

My mom and/or dad or another family member will also come to (location) with me. They will go to a group with other parents and family members to learn about how they can help their kids understand feelings better.

At the Exploring Feelings groups I will meet (names of group leaders). They will be the group leaders. They like to have fun and have worked with young people like me.

First Leader's Name: _____

Second Leader's Name: _____

The first Exploring Feelings group will be on (date) at (time). We will come to the Exploring Feelings group every (day) for (number of) weeks. My group will start at (time) PM and go on for about 2 hours.

Altogether there will be (number of sessions) (day) that we will go to the Exploring Feelings groups. On the first day of the Exploring Feelings group we will wait in the waiting room until (group leaders' names) come to get us. There will be other families waiting, too.

Once all of the families have arrived we will go to a room with (group leaders' names). We will get to meet everyone. To make it easy to remember everyone's names, we'll wear name badges.

We will get some Exploring Feelings worksheets. These will have the activities we will be doing on them.

All the young people will be in one room and all the parents will go into a different room. At the end of each group we will go back to the waiting room to meet the parents or other family members. When we go home we can talk about what was learned in our group, and the tasks to do before next week.

Other young people have come to Exploring Feelings groups and said they have had lots of fun. As well as having fun, these young people have learned more about their feelings and what to do when they feel anxious. I can do these things at my group.

Please come to (location and directions).

(Transportation information)

We look forward to seeing you on (start date). If you need to send a message to us or have any questions before then, you can call (named person) at (telephone number).

General Items:

Refreshments ☐

Pens/pencils ☐

Handbook/loose-leafed folder ☐

Marker pens ☐

Flip chart paper ☐

Stickers to make name badges ☐

Relaxation script ☐

Relaxing music ☐

CD player ☐

Session 1:

Length of rope ☐

Happy words on slips of paper ☐

Blank slips of paper ☐

Session 2:

Handouts from Session 1 ☐

Length of rope ☐

Headings cards ☐

Anxious words cards ☐

Activity sheets for Project Work ☐

Session 3:

Handouts from Session 2 ☐

Session 4:

Handouts from Session 3 ☐

Length of rope ☐

Post-its (12 -15 per participant) ☐

Session 5:

Handouts from Session 4 ☐

List of situations that cause anxiety ☐

Statement cards ☐

Session 6:

Handout from Session 5 ☐

James and the Math Test ☐

Evaluation forms ☐

Certificate of Participation ☐

Being Happy

What makes us feel happy?

| Playing on the computer | Being in bed | Pet rabbit | Being nominated for something | Drama | Wrestling |

What does our body look like when we are happy?

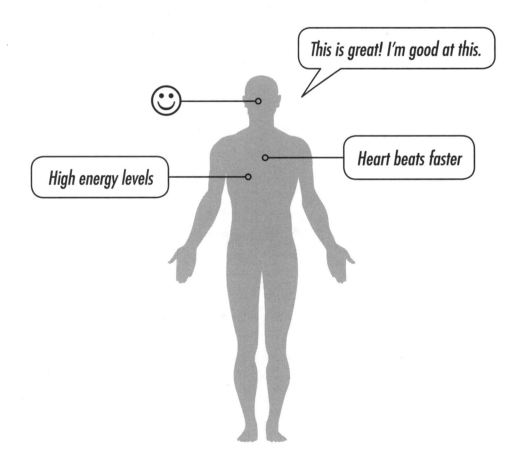

This is great! I'm good at this.

High energy levels

Heart beats faster

People might feel happy or unhappy depending on the situation and what that situation means to them.

For example:

- Getting an A for a school assignment might make you feel happy

- Being scolded by a teacher might make you feel unhappy

Feeling Relaxed?

When do we feel relaxed?

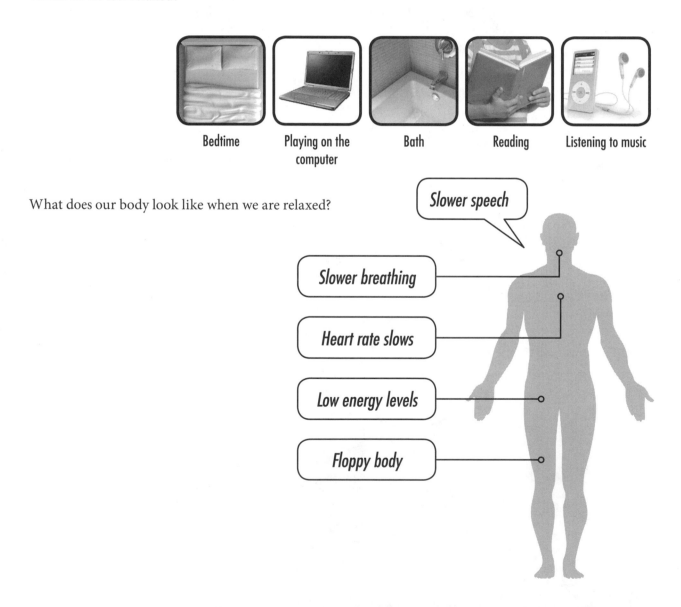

Bedtime   Playing on the computer   Bath   Reading   Listening to music

What does our body look like when we are relaxed?

Slower speech

Slower breathing

Heart rate slows

Low energy levels

Floppy body

How Can We Relax?

Deep breathing

Sit comfortably with your eyes closed. Take a deep, slow breath in through your nose and then slowly let the air out through your mouth.

Breathing slowly in ... out ... in ... out. Imagine that there's a candle in front of you and as you breathe in and out you make the flame flicker.

Imagery

Sit comfortably and close your eyes. Now pretend that you are in one of your favorite places; somewhere that makes you feel happy, peaceful, and safe. Think about the colors you can see, think about what shape things are, the sounds and smells.

Deep muscle relaxation

Work through your body, tensing each group of muscles and then relaxing them in turn.

What does our body look like when we feel anxious?

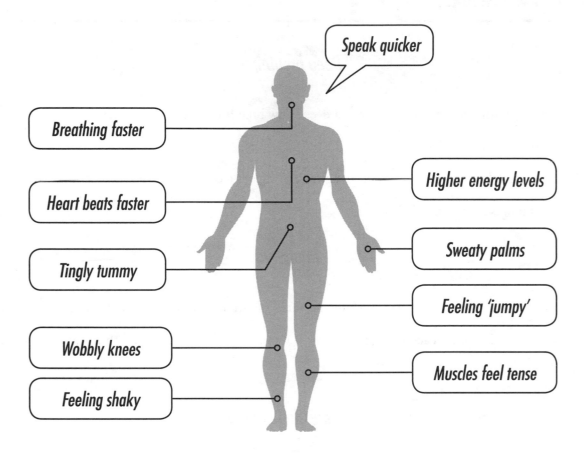

Things that can make us feel anxious:

- First day of school – "Will anyone want to be my friend?"
- "Will I get a good job when I'm older?"
- Using public restrooms
- An important meeting
- Exams / taking a test
- Unsure about something

- Something unexpected happening
- The dark
- "Something bad might happen"
- Having to stand up and talk in front of others
- Dogs
- Dentists

Toolbox to Fix the Feeling of Anxiety

 Playing rugby

 Playing on the computer

 Going to a quiet place

 Writing worries down

 Tidying/cleaning

 Talking to someone

 Dancing

 TV

 Running/walking

 Cooking

 Keeping busy

 Darts

1. Social Tools to Fix the Feeling of Anxiety:

| Joking with someone | Listening to music | Talking to someone | Asking for advice | Making a cup of tea | Making a list |

| Tidying/cleaning | Looking in a book | Running/walking | Change in environment | Relaxation | Watching TV |

2. Thinking Tools to Fix the Feeling of Anxiety

You can tell yourself:

- "It's almost over"
- "Not long now"
- "Calm down"
- "It's just a little thing"
- "Just get on with it"
- "You can do it"
- "I can be brave"

You can also use these thinking ideas:

| Thinking about something else | Thinking about something funny |

3. Unhelpful / Silly Tools

These tools often make you feel more anxious:

- Thinking about the "worst case scenario"—the worst thing that could happen
- Hitting people or objects
- Getting angry
- Talking to someone who is a "big worrier"

Things That Make Us Feel Anxious:

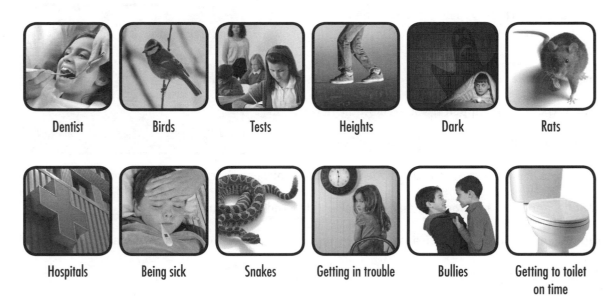

Dentist   Birds   Tests   Heights   Dark   Rats

Hospitals   Being sick   Snakes   Getting in trouble   Bullies   Getting to toilet on time

Different Levels of Anxiety

Different situations can lead to different levels of anxiety.

These situations can be placed on a "thermometer" to show

how anxious they make you feel:

Being on my own   Rides

Taking a test

Going to school

Being told off

You can use the tools you have learned to help you to face these fears.

It is best to start with situations that make you feel a little bit anxious (those at the bottom of the thermometer) and work up to the ones that make you most anxious (at the top of the thermometer).

Why don't you have a go!

Social Stories

Social stories are a short story to help you understand what to do in certain situations.

You may remember in the session we used a comic strip to work through what might happen if you went to the dentist and to draw what you might be thinking, feeling, and doing.

We then drew how you might change your anxious ("poisonous") thoughts to more positive ("antidote") thoughts and how this would change the way you felt and what you might do.

We sent you a copy of this social story for you to use to draw your own social story about a situation that makes you feel anxious.

Antidote to Poisonous Thoughts

We created a list of anxious ("poisonous") thoughts and practiced challenging them with positive ("antidote") thoughts to help reduce your feelings of anxiety.

Here is a list of the thoughts we came up with:

ANXIOUS ("POISONOUS") THOUGHTS 🙁	POSITIVE ("ANTIDOTE") THOUGHTS 🙂
"I always make mistakes"	"Relax, it's only work" "Everyone makes mistakes" "We can learn from our mistakes"
"I am useless at soccer"	"I'll get better next time" "I can practice, and practice makes perfect" "It's not about winning, it's about having fun"
"Everyone hates me"	"So what! I have my own life" "I've got other friends" "Not everybody hates me"

ANXIOUS ("POISONOUS") THOUGHTS ☹	POSITIVE ("ANTIDOTE") THOUGHTS ☺
"I have no friends"	"That's not true, people play with me" "If I asked people, someone would say they were my friend"
"I can't cope!"	"Oh well, it's almost over/I'm not going to feel this way forever" "I've coped with things before" "Think about something I do well"
"I'm going to cry"	"I'm not going to cry, I can cope" "I can think of something happy" "Even if I cry, it's ok"
"The noises are too loud"	"Just go with the flow" "I can think of something else to take my mind off it"
"There's going to be a change"	"I've coped with change before" "It could be a good change, it might make things better" "People can help me with the change"

We set you the task of making your own list of "poisonous" and "antidote" thoughts.

Emotions have a great influence on our bodies and our behavior. Anxiety and frustration can arise from social misunderstanding and make progress very difficult. For example, young people may start to avoid social situations or "blow up" every time they are forced to meet new people.

Identify with your child the bodily feelings that accompany different emotions—note how similar many of the bodily feelings can be, and how this might be confusing if we are unable to state what emotion we are feeling.

Anxiety and frustration/anger can be so overwhelming that the young person is unable to put into action the social skills that they may have developed or possess. For example, a young person may know what to say to peers, but he or she feels so anxious about making the approach that this results in an avoidance of peers or the situation. Moreover, the young person who frequently experiences high levels of frustration or anger may be more likely to react aggressively in an ambiguous or potentially confrontational situation, rather than being able to remain calm enough to utilize their social skills.

Techniques

These all help to bring down emotional level—particularly for anger and anxiety.

Breathing – facilitates relaxation and makes anxiety difficult

Script to be read in a quiet, calm voice when the young person is ready to practice.

Sit comfortably and close your eyes. Concentrate on taking a deep, slow breath in and as you do, feel the air flowing in through your nose. Now, let the air out slowly as you concentrate on breathing out through your mouth. Feel the air flowing out of your mouth. Take another deep breath in, again feeling the air coming in through your nose and then slowly let it out through your mouth. In ... out ... in ... out. While you are concentrating on your breathing, you are starting to feel more and more relaxed. Now I want you to imagine that there is a candle in front of you, and when you breathe in ... and out ... in ... and out ... your breathing makes the flame flicker. Imagine the flame flickering as you slowly breathe in ... and then again as you breathe out. Your breathing is now feeling very, very relaxed and all your worries are draining away with every breath out. In ... and out ... in ... and out ... in ... and out. Now imagine that you blow the candle out and when you are ready, open your eyes.

Talk about how it feels to be relaxed.

Visualizing — utilizes visual learning/thinking cognitive style

This technique is useful since if it is practiced, you can learn to bring up a relaxing image in your head and it has the same effect as doing the breathing.

Sit comfortably and close your eyes. Now, I would like you to pretend that you are in one of your favorite places. Think about somewhere that makes you feel happy, peaceful, and very safe. Now I want you to try and imagine all the details of this safe, peaceful place. Think about the colors you can see, think about what shape things are. Concentrate on all the sounds you can hear and think about what you can smell. Imagine where exactly in this picture you are. You sit down and touch the ground next to you, think about how the ground feels. Are there any other people in the picture with you? Who are they? Now that you have the picture of your safe and peaceful place so clearly in your mind, we can start to concentrate on relaxing our breathing. You are in your peaceful place and you feel calm and safe and happy. You feel so wonderful that you take an enormous breath in and can feel the air rushing in through your nose and filling your lungs. Then, as you let all the air flow out through your mouth, all your worries and concerns disappear. You start to feel more and more relaxed and carefree. As you carry on taking big breaths in and out, and look around in your safe place, all the tension in your muscles starts to drain away and your body starts to feel very relaxed. Still concentrating on your breathing, you start to notice how sweet and fresh the air smells and how good deep breathing is making you feel. Breathe in ... and out ... in ... and out ... in ... and out. Notice how you feel right now. Remember that you can come back to this safe, peaceful, and happy place whenever you want to—when you are feeling anxious or afraid, or angry or frustrated or even when you feel upset about something. When you are in this safe place all your worries disappear so that you can feel relaxed and happy. Take a few more deep breaths in and out and then when you are ready, open your eyes.

The young person may want to draw a picture of their relaxing place.

Muscle Relaxation – may appeal to those children who cannot concentrate on the breathing exercises

We will start at the bottom of our bodies and work up, learning how to relax each part of our body at a time. To learn what it feels like to have relaxed muscles first of all we have to know what it feels like to have tense muscles. So I want you to screw up your toes as tight as you can, that's right really screw them up into little balls, feel how tight your toes and feet feel and hold them really, really tight (hold for about ten seconds) and now let them go – see how relaxed and floppy they feel now. Next I want you to pull your toes back towards your knees as tight as you can. Feel it pulling down the bottom of your legs. Pull them back so they feel really tight and hold it, okay, and now relax your feet again. That's what it's like to have relaxed feet and legs. Now we need to know about the top half of our legs. Press your knees together as tight as you can and push your bottom down hard on the chair or floor. Really feel those muscles in your legs pushing and hold them really tight (hold for ten seconds). Okay, and relax and give your legs a little shake. Now you have totally relaxed legs. Next we will do our tummies. Take a deep breath in and pull your tummy in as tight as you can. Try to make it disappear. Pull it in really, really hard. That's right, hold it tight (for ten seconds) and then relax, feel how comfortable it feels when your body relaxes. Next your arms, make your arms like a muscle man and really show me those muscles. Pull them in really tight until your muscles start to bulge, good, now hold it there (for ten seconds) and relax. Shake your arms out and let them relax completely. Now clench your firsts as tight as you can. Squeeze those fingers in really hard and feel how tight your arms and hands feel. Hold it (for ten seconds) and now let your hands go floppy and relaxed. Now I want you to try and touch your ears with your shoulders. Pull them up as tight as you can and see if you can feel the tightness in your neck and across the top of your back. Hold it tight like that (for ten seconds) and now relax. Let your shoulders slump as the muscles let out all that tension and go floppy. Now we're onto our head. First of all, wrinkle up your nose as tight as you can and hold it (for ten seconds) now let it go and let your face go all droopy and soft. Now push your tongue against the roof of your mouth so that your mouth feels all tense and frozen, push it and hold (for ten seconds) and then relax and feel how nice it is. Clamp your lips together, push them down and try to smile so that you can feel the tightness in your cheeks, hold it there (for ten seconds) and then let all the tension escape. Lastly, just screw up your whole face as tight as you can so that you can feel the muscles pulling all round your head—really screw it up, that's right, and hold it there (for ten seconds) and now let it all go out and see how much calmer your head feels.

Distraction – these methods can prove helpful when the young person with Asperger's Syndrome is uninterested in visualization/breathing

Examples include doing something else (physical exercise, watch TV, listen to music, read, sing, crossword), thinking about a mentally challenging task (math sums), thinking about a happy memory (photo, de-stress box item).

De-stress box – form a "de-stress box" with things that relax you inside it

Show it to your child and ask them to make a similar box—like a shoe box filled with music they like, games they enjoy, pictures of a holiday they liked, etc. Encourage your child to use things from the box to help them to relax. They might want to take a small piece from the box to put in their pocket unobtrusively when they are going somewhere new.

Practice using the emotional toolbox to help in the emotional situation you described.

DAY/TIME	SITUATION: WHAT HAPPENED?	TOOLS USED: WHAT DID YOU DO?	OUTCOME: WERE THE TOOLS SUCCESSFUL?

Sometimes I get worried about things.

Some things that make me worry are _____

_____

_____ .

If I start to feel worried, I need to try to stay calm and think about what I should do.

The things that I can do if I start to feel worried are:

STOP

TAKE SOME DEEP BREATHS

THINK "What do I need to do?"

Some things that help me feel less worried are_____

_____

_____ .

If I need some help to calm down I can _____

_____

_____ .

I will know I feel calm when _____

_____

_____ .

UNHELPFUL THOUGHTS	HELPFUL THOUGHTS

1. What did you hope to get from the group?

   _____

   _____

   _____

2. Was this achieved? *(please circle number on scale)*

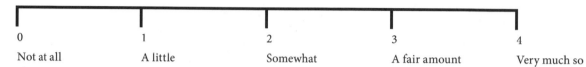

0	1	2	3	4
Not at all	A little	Somewhat	A fair amount	Very much so

   Please comment:

   _____

   _____

   _____

3. What did you hope your child would get from the group?

   _____

   _____

   _____

4. Was this achieved? *(please circle number on scale)*

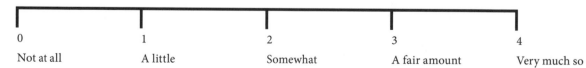

0	1	2	3	4
Not at all	A little	Somewhat	A fair amount	Very much so

5. Do you feel your understanding of anxiety has increased? *(please circle number on scale)*

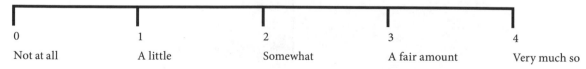

0	1	2	3	4
Not at all	A little	Somewhat	A fair amount	Very much so

6. Do you feel better able to manage your child's anxiety? *(please circle number on scale)*

0	1	2	3	4
Not at all	A little	Somewhat	A fair amount	Very much so

7. Which strategies for managing anxiety have you found most helpful?

_____

_____

_____

8. Has your child's behavior changed? *(please circle number on scale)*

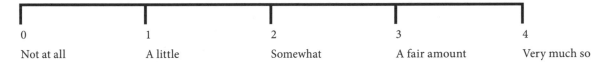

0	1	2	3	4
Not at all	A little	Somewhat	A fair amount	Very much so

If so, how?

_____

_____

_____

9. Would you recommend this group to another family? *(please circle response below)*

YES   NO

10. Any other comments

_____

_____

_____

About the Authors

Dr. Helen Taylor
Clinical Research Associate, Institute of Neuroscience, Newcastle University.

Helen Taylor worked as a highly specialist clinical psychologist in a multidisciplinary child and adolescent mental health service in Newcastle upon Tyne for eleven years, specializing in autism spectrum disorder (ASD) and anxiety. She has recently taken up a position at Newcastle University as clinical research associate on a study examining interventions for eating, drinking, and swallowing difficulties in children with neurodevelopmental difficulties.

Dr. Vicki Grahame
Consultant Clinical Psychologist and Clinical Senior Lecturer, Northumberland, Tyne and Wear NHS Foundation Trust and Newcastle University.

Vicki Grahame is the clinical lead for the nationally commissioned Complex Neurodevelopmental Disorders Service in the northeast of England, which is a specialist tertiary service that provides second opinions about children and young people who may have an Autism Spectrum Disorder (ASD) and other complex mental health or neurodevelopmental problems. She has expertise in the successful planning and delivery of complex intervention trials for children and young people with ASD and their families.

Professor Helen McConachie
Professor of Child Clinical Psychology, Institute of Health and Society, Newcastle University.

Helen McConachie worked for thirty-eight years in multidisciplinary child health and mental health teams, including the National Complex Neurodevelopmental Disorders Service for northeast England. Helen conducts research into appropriate interventions and the measurement of outcomes for individuals on the autism spectrum and their families.

Professor Ann Le Couteur
Professor of Child and Adolescent Psychiatry at Newcastle University and honorary consultant child and Adolescent Psychiatrist for Northumberland, Tyne and Wear NHS Trust.

Ann, until recently, co-led the nationally commissioned Complex Neurodevelopmental Disorders Service (CNDS) based in Newcastle, England. Until this year, she was the UK editor for the Journal of Autism and Developmental Disorders. She chaired the National Autism Plan for children (2003); was an external advisor for the Autism Act (2009) and Statutory Guidance (2010); member of the NICE guidelines for children and young people (2011, 2013); advisor for the evidence updates (2012, 2016), and quality standard (2014).

Dr. Jacqui Rodgers
Senior Lecturer, Clinical Psychology, Institute of Neuroscience, Newcastle University.

Jacqui Rodgers is a senior lecturer and autism researcher in the Institute of Neuroscience, Newcastle University. She leads a program of work which aims to advance the conceptualization, assessment, and treatment of mental health conditions in autism. She is also involved in the development and evaluation of a range of anxiety assessments and intervention programs for children and adults with autism.

Jan O'Neill

Specialist Educational Psychologist (autism), Sunderland Autism Outreach Team.

Jan O'Neill has worked for twenty-one years with children, young people, families, and schools as part of a multi-disciplinary team providing specialist support and training within the Sunderland area.

Dr. Ann Ozsivadjian

Principal Clinical Psychologist, Evelina London Children's Hospital, Guy's and St. Thomas' NHS Foundation Trust.

Ann Ozsivadjian works in the Complex Neurodevelopmental Disabilities team where she has a special interest in the assessment and treatment of mental health difficulties in children and young people with ASD. She has completed a number of research studies in the field. She is also the joint module lead for the first ASD/Intellectual Disability program for the Improving Access to Psychological Therapies (Children and Young People) in the UK.

Dr. Emma Honey

Senior Clinical Psychologist, Northumberland, Tyne and Wear NHS Foundation Trust

Emma Honey has over fifteen years of experience working with children and young people with Autism Spectrum Disorder. She works clinically in the northeast of England in the Complex Neurodevelopmental Disorders Service. She has research interests in the development of interventions for individuals with ASD and in the development and adaptation of appropriate measurement tools.

Dr. Kate Sofronoff

Clinical Psychologist and Associate Professor, University of Queensland, Australia.

Kate is an associate professor on academic staff in the School of Psychology at the University of Queensland, Australia. Kate's main area of research is in evaluating and extending the evidence base for programs aimed to assist children on the autism spectrum and their families.